Holy Stars!
Favorite DEITIES, PROPHETS, SAINTS & SAGES FROM Around THE World!

★

KATHLEEN EDWARDS

SENTIENT PUBLICATIONS

First Sentient Publications edition 2009
Copyright © 2009 by Kathleen Edwards

All rights reserved. This book, or parts thereof, may not be reproduced in any form without permission, except in the case of brief quotations embodied in critical articles and reviews.

A paperback original

Cover design by Kathleen Edwards and Kim Johansen, Black Dog Design
Book design by Adam Schnitzmeier

Library of Congress Cataloging-in-Publication Data

Edwards, Kathleen, 1955-
  Holy stars! : favorite deities, prophets, saints & sages / Kathleen Edwards. -- 1st Sentient Publications ed.
      p. cm.
   ISBN 978-1-59181-080-3 (alk. paper)
 1. Gods. 2. Prophets. 3. Saints. I. Title.
  BL473.E34 2009
  202'.1--dc22
                               2008053078

Printed in the United States of America

10 9 8 7 6 5 4 3 2 1

SENTIENT PUBLICATIONS
A Limited Liability Company
1113 Spruce Street
Boulder, CO 80302
www.sentientpublications.com

Contents

Introduction — 2

Allah — 4
Baha'u'llah — 6
Buddha — 8
Chango — 10
Confucius — 12
Fatima — 14
Gaia — 16
Ganesh — 18
Guardian Angel — 20
Guru Nanak Dev — 22
Jesus — 24
Kali — 26
Krishna — 28
Kuan Yin — 30
Lakshmi — 32
Lao Tzu — 34
Mary — 36
Moses — 38
Muhammad — 40
Pele — 42
Shiva — 44
St. Francis of Assisi — 46
Tara — 48
Virgin of Guadalupe — 50
Yahweh — 52
Yemaya — 54
Zarathustra — 56

Glossary — 58
Resources — 59
About the Author — 60

to my parents, Alan and Madeleine Edwards,
in gratitude for a strong foundation

and

for Ceanna and Kyla

> IF A TEMPLE, OR A SYMBOL, OR AN IMAGE HELPS YOU TO REALIZE THE DIVINE WITHIN, YOU ARE WELCOME TO IT. HAVE TWO HUNDRED IMAGES IF YOU LIKE.... WHATEVER BRINGS YOU NEARER TO GOD. BUT DO NOT QUARREL ABOUT THEM: THE MOMENT YOU QUARREL, YOU ARE NOT GOING GODWARD; YOU ARE GOING BACKWARD TOWARD THE BRUTES.

SWAMI VIVEKANANDA
HINDU SAGE • 1863-1902

Acknowledgments

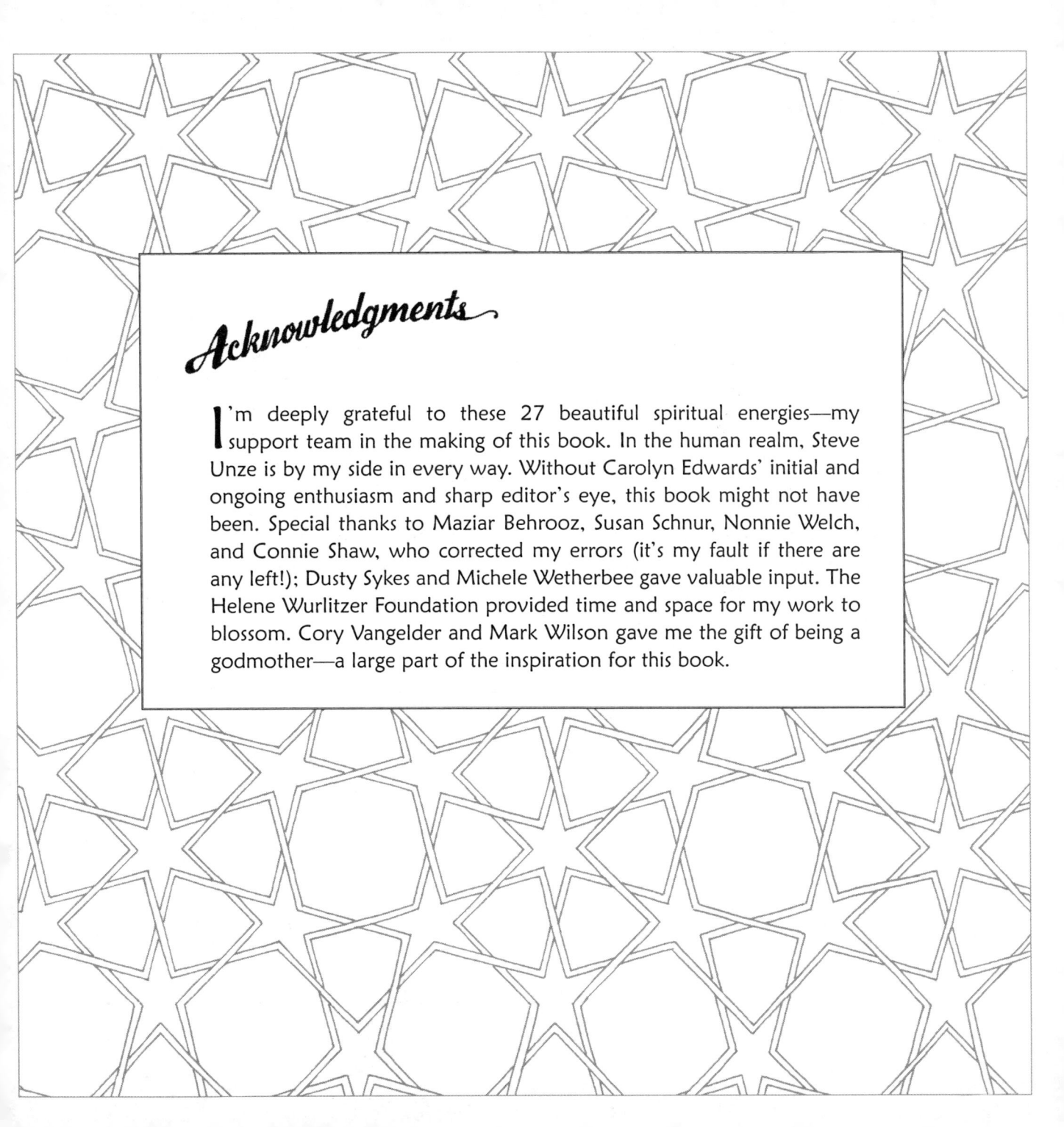

I'm deeply grateful to these 27 beautiful spiritual energies—my support team in the making of this book. In the human realm, Steve Unze is by my side in every way. Without Carolyn Edwards' initial and ongoing enthusiasm and sharp editor's eye, this book might not have been. Special thanks to Maziar Behrooz, Susan Schnur, Nonnie Welch, and Connie Shaw, who corrected my errors (it's my fault if there are any left!); Dusty Sykes and Michele Wetherbee gave valuable input. The Helene Wurlitzer Foundation provided time and space for my work to blossom. Cory Vangelder and Mark Wilson gave me the gift of being a godmother—a large part of the inspiration for this book.

Introduction

"The only stuff that's real is what I can hear, see, smell, taste, and touch!" say some people.

"I believe in invisible forces that are greater than humans but I don't need to name them. I don't need a religion," say others.

Yet for many people religion is an essential and enriching part of life. Deities, teachers, and stories are the tools religions use to make sense of the world's mysteries.

Is religion "real"? The gods, goddesses, prophets, saints, and sages from cultures all over the world might say: "We're *here*! We are not going away! We help people get through their days. We help when they're suffering—even though some folks might wonder why we can't just stop the suffering! But we are here to remind people of the unseen, spiritual dimension of life. Even if we *are* only figments of human imagination, we share life on this planet with all the other earthlings and all the other figments—like dreams, stories, and ideas. We *affect* people's lives and actions. Isn't that *real* enough?!"

In today's world, whether or not we revere religious figures, we hear about and see them all the time. In order to be educated world citizens, it is important to have at least some religious literacy. This book's purpose is to add to that cause.

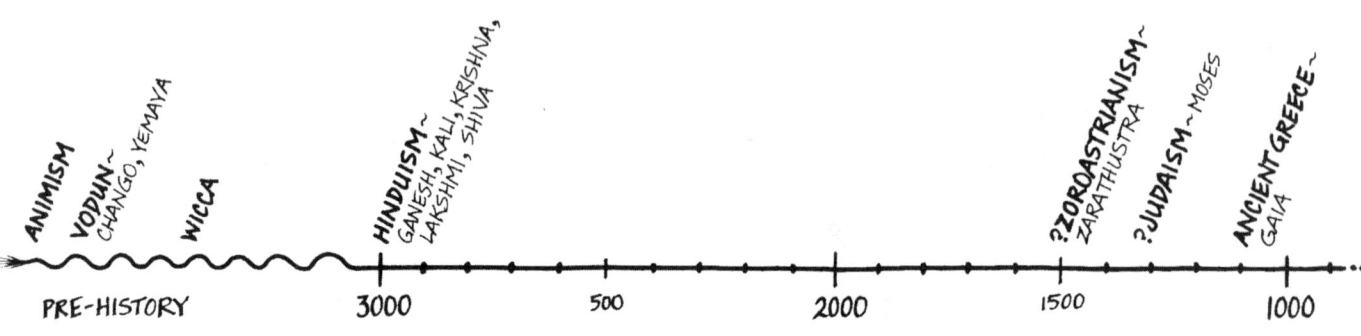

There are thousands upon thousands of revered figures from earth's cultures. I chose figures to include in this book based on those most heard of by North Americans (with an eye towards diversity); those revered by large numbers of people; and those whose name you might read in a newspaper, or whose image you might see on the dashboard of a taxi or in a framed portrait on a living room wall. The religions that got more coverage are those that tend to revere particular deities or individuals; many religions do not. But choosing which figures to include was a bit like doing party invitations. (If I include Alfie I'll *have* to invite Omega.) No matter whom I included or left out, someone is bound to be offended. If so, I apologize in advance.

People of some religions would argue that their deity is the most powerful or the only true one, and that therefore He should not have been included with all these other characters. But this book's purpose is *information*; there is no hierarchy here. In this book, everyone lines up in alphabetical order.

This book is an overview intended to inspire curiosity about the world's wisdom traditions, rather than a comparative survey of religions. Anyone interested in knowing more may get started by using the glossary (italicized words can be found there) and list of resources at the back.

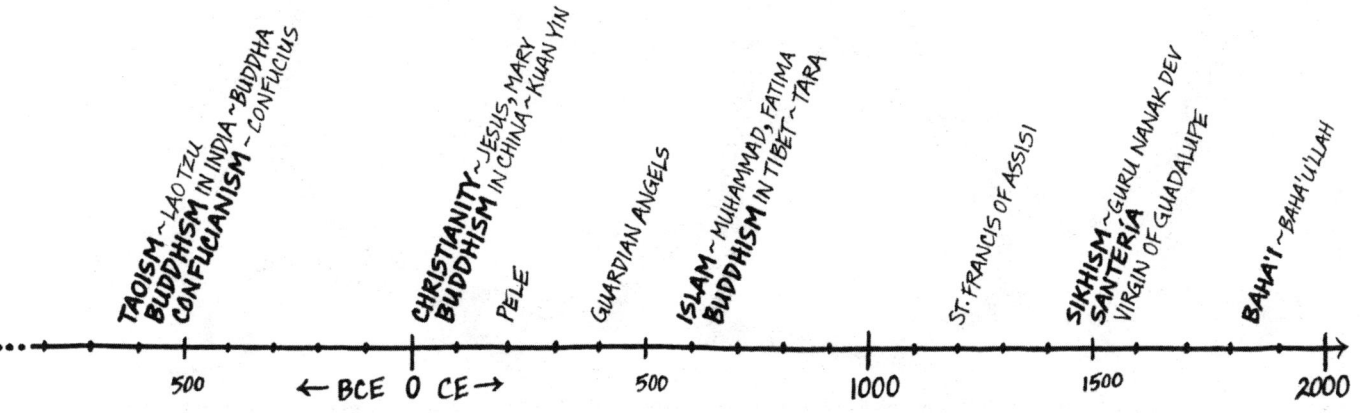

Bahá'u'lláh

MEANS "GLORY OF GOD"

1817–1892
PERSIA
(IRAN)

THE **BAHA'I** RELIGION BEGAN AS A NEW FORM OF ISLAM, INSPIRED BY A SHIITE MUSLIM CALLED **THE BAB**. FOR CLAIMING HE WAS A MANIFESTATION OF GOD, HE WAS EXECUTED IN 1850. ONE OF HIS LOYAL FOLLOWERS, MIRZA HUSAYN ALI NURI ~ LATER CALLED **BAHA'U'LLAH** ~ WAS IMPRISONED IN A NOTORIOUS DUNGEON...

SYMBOL OF BAHA'I

"LISTEN! MIRZA! I AM THE ONE GOD BEHIND ALL FAITHS! ALL MANIFESTATIONS OF ME ARE LIKE RAYS OF THE **SUN** ~ ONE **LIGHT**! RESPECT ALL SCRIPTURES BUT UNDERSTAND THEM IN THE LIGHT OF NEW INSIGHTS! NOW MIRZA: BE A **RAY**!"

FREED AFTER 4 MONTHS, HE WROTE MANY BOOKS, INCLUDING THE *KITAB-I-AQDAS*, THE "MOST HOLY BOOK" OF BAHA'I.

"I AM BAHA'U'LLAH, THE NEW PROPHET THE *BAB* PREDICTED! REVELATIONS SENT FROM **GOD** TO ADAM, ABRAHAM, BUDDHA, KRISHNA, MOSES, JESUS, MUHAMMAD, THE BAB ~ & NOW ME ~ HAVE EACH BEEN PERFECT FOR THEIR TIME. NOW LET US SPREAD **UNITY**!..."

THE UNIVERSE ETERNAL IS GOD'S PERFECT EMANATION, AND ALL THE WORLD'S RELIGIONS ARE TRUTHFUL REVELATIONS.

· ~ ·

HONORING THE LIGHT OF GOD IS THE TASK OF EVERY SOUL. HUMANITY'S ONE FAMILY, WITH PEACE ON EARTH THE GOAL.

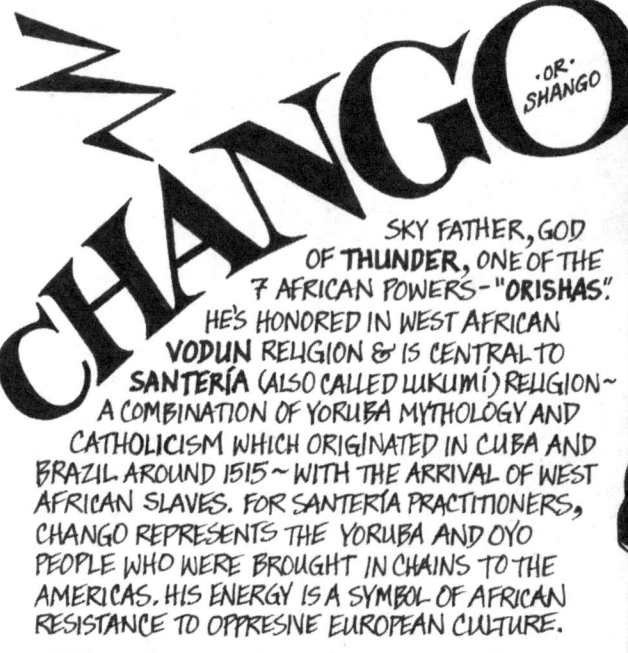

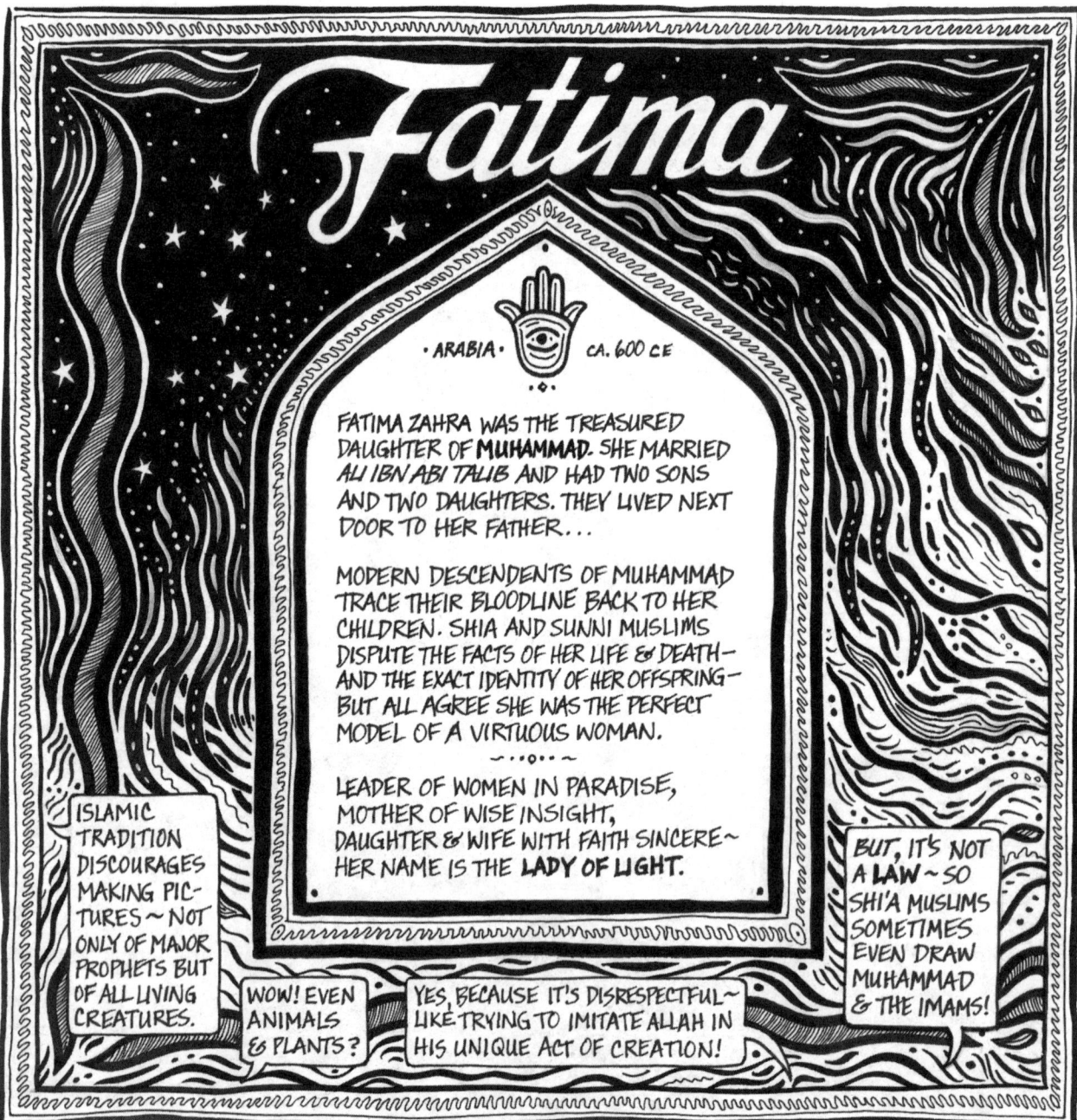

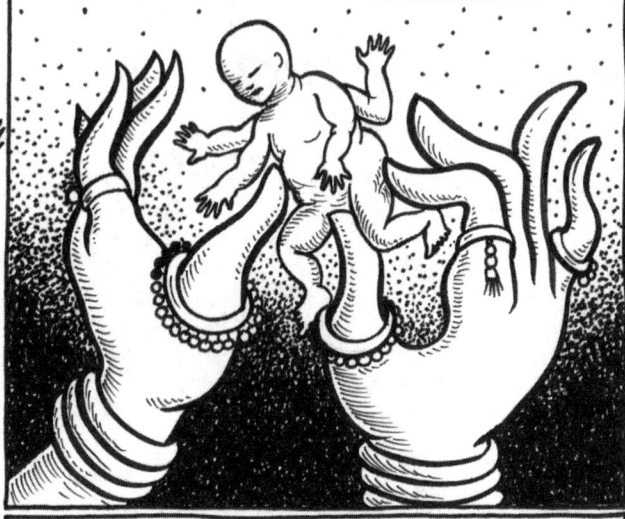

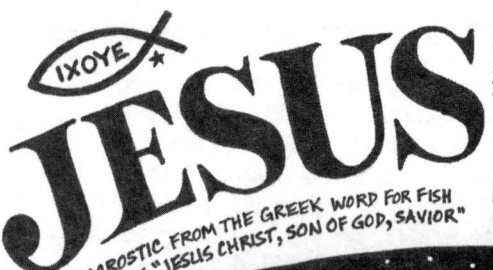

JESUS

*An acrostic from the Greek word for fish that says "Jesus Christ, Son of God, Savior"

CHRIST IS THE CENTRAL FIGURE IN **CHRISTIANITY**. HE'S "GOD THE SON" OF THE HOLY TRINITY ALONG WITH "GOD THE FATHER" (SEE YAWEH) AND "GOD THE HOLY SPIRIT." CHURCHES INCLUDE ROMAN CATHOLIC (WHO REVERE THE POPE), EASTERN ORTHODOX, ANGLICAN & PROTESTANT ~ BAPTIST, METHODIST, PRESBYTERIAN, LUTHERAN & MANY MORE. MORMONS – "LATTER DAY SAINTS" – ARE CHRISTIANS TOO, BUT ALSO FOLLOW 19TH CENTURY AMERICAN PROPHET JOSEPH SMITH JR.

IN BETHLEHEM'S HUMBLE STABLE VIRGIN MARY GAVE BIRTH TO GOD'S SON. THAT NIGHT THE ANGELS SANG PRAISES FOR THE **LIGHT** HAD FINALLY COME!

IT'S THE FIRST CHRISTMAS!

JESUS PERFORMED GREAT MIRACLES LIKE HEALING THE LAME & THE BLIND & MAKING 2 FISH & 5 LOAVES OF BREAD ENOUGH FOR THOUSANDS TO DINE!

HIS POWER THREATENED THE GOVERNMENT SO THEY HAD HIM *CRUCIFIED*. HE CARRIED ALL THE PEOPLE'S SINS TO FREE THEM WHEN HE DIED.

AFTER 3 DAYS IN A TOMB, JESUS ROSE FROM THE DEAD & ASCENDED TO HEAVEN.

ONE DAY I SHALL RETURN AS THE MESSIAH!

EASTER CELEBRATES REBIRTH & SPRING – WE SYMBOLIZE FERTILITY!

THE FIRST EASTER!

KALI

• OFTEN CALLED KALI-MA •

SHE REPRESENTS THE EVERLASTING CYCLE OF **CHANGE**. HER NAME COMES FROM THE *SANSKRIT* WORD "KAL" WHICH MEANS **TIME**. SHE'S HINDUISM'S TRIPLE GODDESS ~ THE CREATOR OF ALL LIFE, THE MOTHER OF ENDLESS LOVE AND THE EVENTUAL DESTROYER OF ALL. SHE'S OFTEN SEEN AS THE GODDESS OF DEATH ~ BUT **NOT** JUST DEATH OF THE **BODY**...

ROT, DECOMPOSITION, VULTURES, MOLD, DEATH, DISINTEGRATION, ROT, AGING, ENTROPY, BACTERIA, DECAY, WORMS, RUST, DISEASE, FUNGUS, MILDEW, ACCIDENTS, FADING

HEY! GIFTS FROM KALI! WITHOUT THEM THERE'D BE NO LIFE!

SHE LIBERATES THE MIND BY DESTROYING ILLUSION ~ "AWAY WITH YOU", SHE CRIES TO LIMITS & CONFUSION!

SHE RELEASES ATTACHMENTS & SLASHES THROUGH IMPURITIES ~ HER RUTHLESSNESS PROVIDES **SPIRITUAL OPPORTUNITIES**!

HAND IN HAND WITH **TIME**, SHARP & SWIFT HER TALENTS, SHE CUTS HUMANITY'S BONDS, & KEEPS THE WORLD IN **BALANCE**!

O! KALI-MA! SLAY THE FEARS THAT LIMIT MY SPIRIT! O! KALI-MA! DANCE ON THE GRAVE OF MY AMBIVALENCE!
~ PRAYER TO KALI

Kuan Yin

Buddhist and Taoist people everywhere ~ in homes & hospitals, shipboard & in shops ~ pray to Kuan Yin, the Chinese *bodhisattva* of compassion, Mother of Mercy, she who **hears the cries of the world**.

...WAS ONCE THE DAUGHTER OF A CRUEL KING...

"YOU WILL MARRY THE RICH MAN I CHOOSE FOR YOU!"

"NO. I WON'T MARRY. I WANT ONLY HEALING FOR ALL."

LATER, WHEN HE SAW THE BIRDS, ANIMALS & EVEN THE FIRE WERE HELPING HER WITH THE WORK HE'D ORDERED HER TO DO AS PUNISHMENT, HE CALLED FOR AN EXECUTIONER...

WHEN THE EXECUTIONER COULD **NOT** KILL HER, KUAN YIN RODE ON THE BACK OF A TIGER TO MEET LONELY SOULS IN THE **LAND OF THE DEAD**...

THERE SHE RELEASED ALL THE GOOD *KARMA* SHE'D ACCUMULATED THROUGHOUT MANY LIFETIMES AND FREED THE LONELY SOULS BACK TO EARTH & HEAVEN.

MEANWHILE, HER FATHER LAY DYING, VISITED BY A DOCTOR...

"NOTHING WILL CURE YOU EXCEPT THE EYE OF SOMEONE WHO SEES THE WORLD WITH **MERCY**."

ON FRAGRANT MOUNTAIN, THE KING'S SERVANT FOUND AN OLD HERMIT WHO PLUCKED OUT HIS **EYE** TO GIVE TO THE KING.

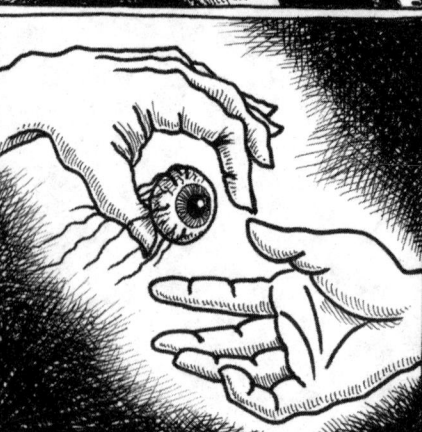

WHEN THE KING WENT TO THANK THE HERMIT FOR SAVING HIS LIFE, THE OLD MAN'S BODY FELL AWAY ~ AND THERE STOOD KUAN YIN...

"HOW COULD YOU HAVE DONE THIS FOR ME?"

"I NEVER REST UNTIL ALL BEINGS ARE FREE OF IGNORANCE & SUFFERING."

Lakshmi

HINDU GODDESS OF **FORTUNE** & **WEALTH**, BOTH WORLDLY & SPIRITUAL, SHE EMBODIES BEAUTY, GRACE & CHARM. SHE IS ALSO ONE OF INDIA'S **MOTHER** GODDESSES.

* * * * *

ONCE UPON AN ANCIENT TIME, LAKSHMI AROSE FROM THE COSMIC SEA OF MILK, A RED LOTUS HELD HIGH IN HER HAND. EACH OF THE DIVINE HINDU TRINITY ~ BRAHMA (CREATOR), VISHNU (PRESERVER), SHIVA (DESTROYER) ~ WERE DAZZLED BY HER BEAUTY...

"I SHALL BE VISHNU'S PARTNER! AND IN THE *RAMAYANA* I SHALL BE SITA, WIFE TO RAMA— VISHNU'S AVATAR!"

THE LOTUS IS A COMMON SYMBOL IN BOTH HINDU AND BUDDHIST ICONOGRAPHY. LAKSHMI IN PARTICULAR IS ASSOCIATED WITH IT.

"I AM ROOTED IN **MUD**: THE FINITE WORLD OF PHYSICAL EXISTENCE. MY BLOOMS RISE ABOVE IN UNCONTAMINATED BEAUTY: SPIRITUAL PERFECTION & AUTHORITY."

"I AM THE WET SOIL'S FERTILITY, THE MYSTERY OF GROWTH & THE TRANSCENDENT FLOWERING OF SPIRITUALITY!"

Favorite of women, good luck she brings, her comfort arrives on prosperity's wings!

PEOPLE HONOR LAKSHMI ~ ESPECIALLY IN THEIR HOMES ~ WHERE THEY PRAY FOR THE WELL-BEING OF THE FAMILY. BUSINESSPEOPLE PLACE HER IMAGE INSIDE THEIR WALLETS OR STICK IT ON THEIR COMPUTERS ~ TALISMANS FOR **GOOD FORTUNE**!

"LAKSHMI IS OFTEN SHOWN WITH ME, FOR WE ARE BOTH GODS OF **ABUNDANCE**!"

MY FOUR HANDS SYMBOLIZE THE FOUR BLESSINGS OF HUMAN EXISTENCE: **DHARMA**~RIGHTEOUS ACTS; **ARTHA**~WEALTH; **KAMA**~SENSUAL PLEASURE; **MOKSHA**~FINAL LIBERATION.
THE BIGGEST OF ALL HINDU FESTIVALS IS 4-DAY **DIVALI**-THE FESTIVAL OF LIGHTS. ON THE SECOND DAY SPECIAL HONOR IS GIVEN TO LAKSHMI.
I BOW TO YOU, O LAKSHMI, MOTHER OF ALL WORLDS, LOTUS BORN, REPOSING IN THE BOSOM OF VISHNU... GOOD HEALTH, PROSPERITY & HAPPINESS ARE NOT HARD TO ATTAIN FOR THOSE ON WHOM YOU BESTOW YOUR KINDNESS... PLEASE NEVER LEAVE OUR WEALTH AND LIVELIHOODS; OUR HOMES, BODIES, FAMILIES, FRIENDS & ANIMALS.
~PRAYER TO LAKSHMI

Lao Tzu

LAO TZU MEANS "OLD SAGE" OR "OLD MASTER." IN 16TH CENTURY B.C.E. CHINA, HE WROTE THE **TAO TE CHING**, SECOND ONLY TO THE BIBLE AS THE WORLD'S MOST TRANSLATED BOOK. THESE TEACHINGS ARE THE BASIS OF **TAOISM**, A PHILOSOPHY & RELIGIOUS SYSTEM INFLUENCED BY NATURE. WITHOUT GODS OR STRICT RULES, IT SUGGESTS HOW TO LIVE A LIFE OF COMPASSION AND PEACE.

LAO TZU WROTE HIS BESTSELLER AT THE AGE OF 80! AFTER RETIRING AS AN ARCHIVIST AT THE IMPERIAL COURT, HE LEFT HOME ON HIS FAVORITE WATER BUFFALO...

> I AM **SO** DISILLUSIONED THAT MOST PEOPLE WON'T SEEK A PATH TO GOODNESS. **HMPH.** I'M MOVING TO THE DESERT TO LIVE IN SOLITUDE.

> AH... THE LAST GATE OUT OF THE KINGDOM...

> WAIT! LAO TZU!

> BEFORE YOU GO! I'V HEARD OF YOUR TEACHINGS. PLEASE WRITE THEM DOWN SO I CAN SHARE THEM...

> HMM... WELL... ALL RIGHT. LET ME FIND MY PEN AND MY SCROLL...

"TAO" MEANS THE WAY OF ALL LIFE...
SIMPLICITY IS THE KEY.
OBSERVING THE LAWS OF NATURE...
ALLOWING YOURSELF TO **BE**...

THE SOFTEST THINGS IN THE WORLD OVERCOME THE HARDEST THINGS IN THE WORLD.
BE CONTENT WITH WHAT YOU HAVE; REJOICE IN THE WAY THINGS ARE. WHEN YOU REALIZE THERE IS NOTHING LACKING, THE WHOLE WORLD BELONGS TO YOU.
VIOLENCE, EVEN WELL INTENTIONED, ALWAYS REBOUNDS UPON ONESELF.
SILENCE IS A SOURCE OF GREAT STRENGTH.
A GOOD TRAVELER HAS NO FIXED PLANS AND IS NOT INTENT ON ARRIVING...
YIN YANG SYMBOL: HARMONY & BALANCE

Mary

First there was the **Annunciation** ~ the announcement...

"I'm Gabriel, the angel! Mary, you're going to give birth to baby Jesus."

"But... how...? I'm a virgin!"

"...Conceived by the Holy Spirit!"

"But my fiancé Joseph will be very upset!"

"He'll be fine. Trust me."

SEE ALSO: VIRGIN OF GUADALUPE

Just as the angel foretold, Mary gave birth to God's son, Jesus. Lovingly, Mary and Joseph raised him, watching him grow into the great teacher who would found a new religion. (See Jesus)

Since the Middle Ages, Mary has been called **Madonna** — which means "my lady"

The Assumption

Queen of Heaven is what she's called for by legend she didn't die ~ but ascended directly to paradise where she graces the heavenly sky!

★ ★ ★

The **Feast** of the **Assumption** is celebrated in many countries.

36

"HAIL MARY, FULL OF GRACE, THE LORD IS WITH YOU; BLESSED ARE YOU AMONG WOMEN & BLESSED IS THE FRUIT OF YOUR WOMB, JESUS. HOLY MARY, MOTHER OF GOD, PRAY FOR US SINNERS, NOW & AT THE HOUR OF OUR DEATH. AMEN.
—HAIL MARY ROSARY PRAYER

MANY CATHEDRALS OF EUROPE DEDICATED TO "OUR LADY"—MARY—WERE BUILT OVER ANCIENT *PAGAN* SHRINES TO GODDESSES!

SO...HONORING THE SACRED FEMININE HAS BEEN KEPT *ALIVE*!

THE **IMMACULATE CONCEPTION**: SOME CHRISTIANS BELIEVE THAT BECAUSE MARY WAS TO BE THE MOTHER OF GOD'S SON, SHE WAS EXEMPT FROM ORIGINAL SIN FROM THE MOMENT SHE WAS CONCEIVED.

AND HEY... MUSLIMS HONOR MARY TOO!

MOSES
CA. 1200 BCE

HEBREW PROPHET, AUTHOR OF THE *TORAH*, THE EARLY HISTORY OF THE JEWISH PEOPLE; AND BRINGER OF *MONOTHEISM* TO THEIR THEN *POLYTHEISTIC* SOCIETY.
HE IS REVERED AS A MAJOR PROPHET BY JEWS, CHRISTIANS, MUSLIMS AND BAHÁ'ÍS.

WHEN MOSES WAS BORN TO A HEBREW SLAVE FAMILY IN EGYPT, THE PHARAOH (KING) HAD MADE A NEW LAW....

I DECREE! ALL HEBREW MALES ARE TO BE KILLED AT BIRTH!

TO SAVE HER SON, MOSES' MOTHER PUT HIM IN A WATERPROOF BASKET AND SET HIM AFLOAT IN THE NILE RIVER...

PHARAOH'S DAUGHTER WAS BATHING ON THE RIVERBANK...

OOH! SWEET BABY! ARE YOU LOST, LITTLE ONE? I'LL BRING YOU HOME!

...AND SO HE WAS RAISED AS A STRONG & CONFIDENT EGYPTIAN PRINCE!

LIVING IN A WORLD OF SLAVES & MASTERS, HE GREW UP TO FIGHT INJUSTICE. ONE NIGHT *GOD* APPEARED TO HIM AS A BURNING BUSH! (SEE YAHWEH)

MOSES! LEAD MY PEOPLE OUT OF SLAVERY INTO A NEW LAND!

AM I WORTHY? CAN I DO THIS? I MUST TRUST.

TO SHAKE UP PHARAOH, GOD SENT TEN PLAGUES TO EGYPT - THE LAST ONE THE DEATH OF MALE FIRST-BORNS. IT "PASSED OVER" HEBREW HOUSES; JEWS REMEMBER THESE EVENTS AT *PASSOVER*.

ALL RIGHT! ENOUGH! YOU'RE FREE! GO!

LEADING HIS PEOPLE THROUGH DESERT, BEING GOD'S HANDS AND FEET - HE FED THE HUNGRY TRAVELERS, MADE BITTER WATER SWEET!
....
MOSES CLIMBED A MOUNTAINTOP TO HEAR WHAT GOD HAD TO SAY: "HERE ARE MY 10 COMMANDMENTS TO GUIDE YOU ON YOUR WAY."

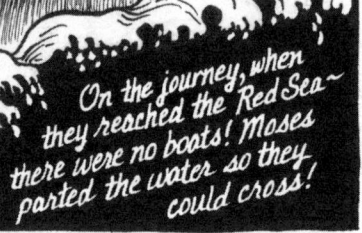

On the journey, when they reached the Red Sea ~ there were no boats! Moses parted the water so they could cross!

38

the Ten Commandments

1. I AM THE LORD THY GOD. THOU SHALT HAVE NO OTHER GODS BEFORE ME.
2. THOU SHALT NOT MAKE IDOLS.
3. THOU SHALT NOT MISUSE GOD'S NAME.
4. REMEMBER THE SABBATH & KEEP IT HOLY.
5. HONOR THY FATHER & THY MOTHER.
6. THOU SHALT NOT MURDER.
7. THOU SHALT NOT COMMIT ADULTERY.
8. THOU SHALT NOT STEAL.
9. THOU SHALT NOT LIE.
10. THOU SHALT NOT DESIRE WHAT BELONGS TO THY NEIGHBOR.

THE **TORAH** IS THE FIRST FIVE BOOKS OF THE HEBREW SCRIPTURES. (CHRISTIANS CALL THAT THE OLD TESTAMENT.) THE **TALMUD** IS THE ANCIENT RABBINICAL WRITINGS THAT GUIDE ORTHODOX JEWS.

IN JUDAISM, ARE **PICTURES** OF PROPHETS OKAY?

IT'S OK IN A STORYBOOK BUT NOT IN A TEMPLE. NO IMAGE SHOULD BE MORE IMPORTANT THAN GOD!

Muhammad

...IN ARABIC SCRIPT:

> ALLAH HAS REVEALED TO ME THAT YOU SHOULD ADOPT HUMILITY SO THAT NO ONE OPPRESSES ANOTHER...
> —FROM "HADITH," SAYINGS OF MUHAMMAD

WHAT IS RAMADAN?

IT CELEBRATES THE REVELATION OF THE QUR'AN TO MUHAMMAD AND IS A MONTH OF FASTING, PURIFICATION AND REDEDICATION OF ONESELF TO GOD.

...AND ID-UL-FITR IS A JOYFUL 4-DAY HOLIDAY MARKING RAMADAN'S END!

...THIS IS A TILEWORK DESIGN FROM A VERY OLD MOSQUE IN SAMARKAND, UZBEKISTAN...

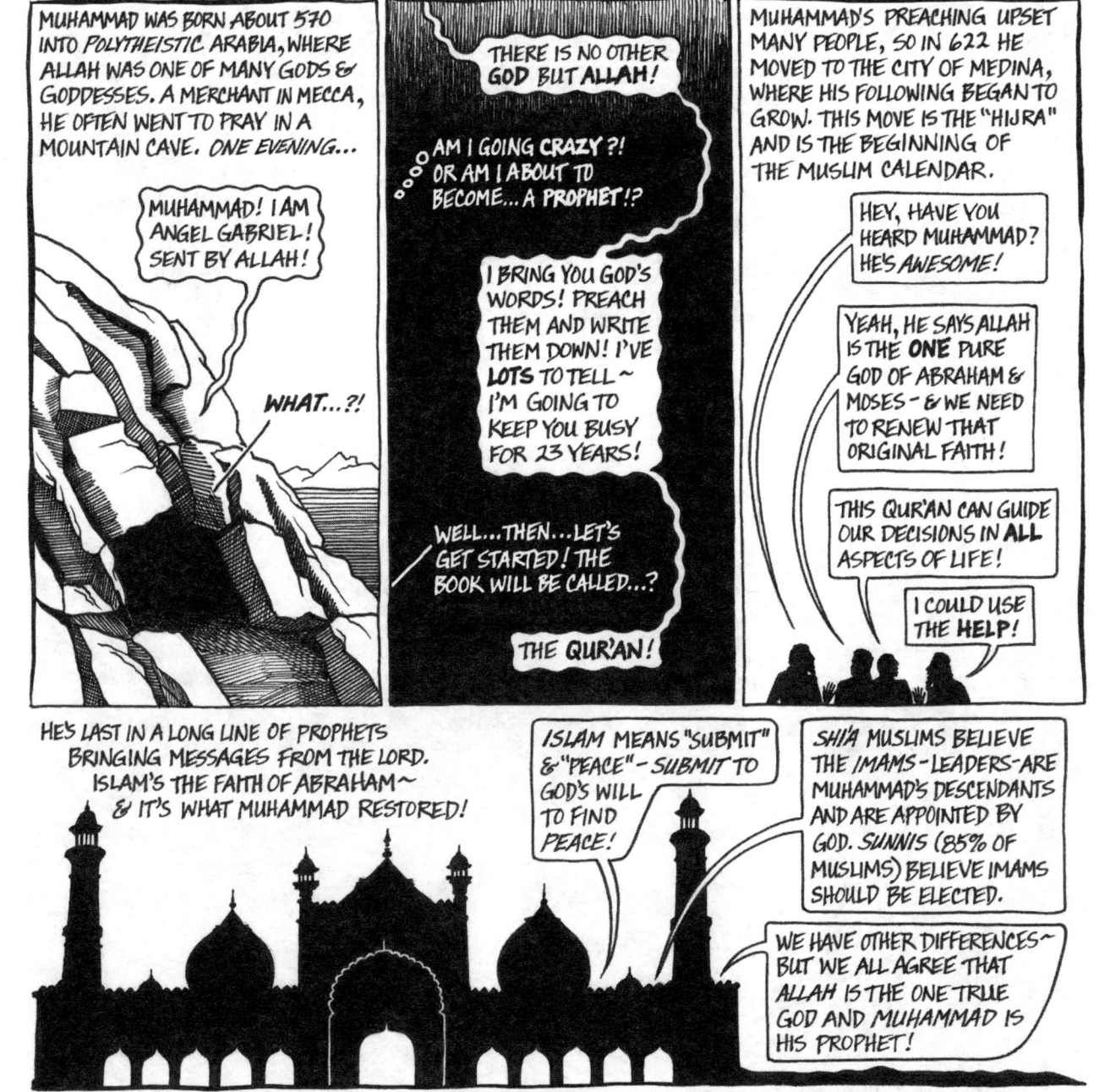
MUHAMMAD WAS BORN ABOUT 570 INTO *POLYTHEISTIC* ARABIA, WHERE ALLAH WAS ONE OF MANY GODS & GODDESSES. A MERCHANT IN MECCA, HE OFTEN WENT TO PRAY IN A MOUNTAIN CAVE. *ONE EVENING...*
MUHAMMAD! I AM ANGEL GABRIEL! SENT BY ALLAH!
WHAT...?!
THERE IS NO OTHER **GOD** BUT **ALLAH**!
AM I GOING **CRAZY**?! OR AM I ABOUT TO BECOME... A **PROPHET**!?
I BRING YOU GOD'S WORDS! PREACH THEM AND WRITE THEM DOWN! I'VE **LOTS** TO TELL ~ I'M GOING TO KEEP YOU BUSY FOR 23 YEARS!
WELL... THEN... LET'S GET STARTED! THE BOOK WILL BE CALLED...?
THE **QUR'AN**!
MUHAMMAD'S PREACHING UPSET MANY PEOPLE, SO IN 622 HE MOVED TO THE CITY OF MEDINA, WHERE HIS FOLLOWING BEGAN TO GROW. THIS MOVE IS THE "HIJRA" AND IS THE BEGINNING OF THE MUSLIM CALENDAR.
HEY, HAVE YOU HEARD MUHAMMAD? HE'S *AWESOME*!
YEAH, HE SAYS ALLAH IS THE **ONE** PURE GOD OF ABRAHAM & MOSES - & WE NEED TO RENEW THAT ORIGINAL FAITH!
THIS QUR'AN CAN GUIDE OUR DECISIONS IN **ALL** ASPECTS OF LIFE!
I COULD USE THE **HELP**!
HE'S *LAST* IN A LONG LINE OF PROPHETS BRINGING MESSAGES FROM THE LORD. ISLAM'S THE FAITH OF ABRAHAM ~ & IT'S WHAT MUHAMMAD RESTORED!
ISLAM MEANS "SUBMIT" & "PEACE" - *SUBMIT* TO GOD'S WILL TO FIND *PEACE*!
SHI'A MUSLIMS BELIEVE THE *IMAMS* - LEADERS - ARE MUHAMMAD'S DESCENDANTS AND ARE APPOINTED BY GOD. *SUNNIS* (85% OF MUSLIMS) BELIEVE IMAMS SHOULD BE ELECTED.
WE HAVE OTHER DIFFERENCES ~ BUT WE ALL AGREE THAT *ALLAH* IS THE ONE TRUE GOD AND *MUHAMMAD* IS HIS PROPHET!

Pele

Once upon an ancient time in Tahiti, sky god Kane Milohai and earth goddess Haumea gave birth to fiery daughter **PELE**.... Fleeing her angry ocean goddess sister, Pele set forth in a canoe to find a new home. Arriving in beautiful **HAWAII**, she wandered the islands, finally landing at Mauna Kea on the Big Island. With a deep sense of homecoming, she dug her **HALEMA'UMA'U CRATER** at the heart of **KILAUEA** volcano, where she lives to this day!

> From Tahiti, close to her heart, Pele carried a precious egg that became her youngest sister: I, Hi'iaka. It was I who first swayed gracefully in my magic skirt, beginning the dance of **HULA**. These movements & chants—"MELE"—are spiritual offerings & praise to spirits of earth, air, fire, water & the ancestor gods.

> Native Hawaiians offer flower leis & food wrapped in ti leaves at the volcano's crater to honor Pele. Thunder & pouring rain are signs the offerings have been accepted.

The raging of Pele can be heard
In the pit of Halema'uma'u
The heavens flash on & on
The heavens flash on & on
May a deep respect come to us
May a deep respect come to us
O Pele
O Pele
In the name of Pele
~Chant to Pele

LEGEND SAYS THAT TAKING LAVA ROCKS OR SAND FROM HAWAII BRINGS BAD LUCK. NATIVE HAWAIIANS BELIEVE EVERY ROCK HOLDS POWER & SHOULDN'T BE STOLEN FROM PELE! OFTEN ADDRESSED TO "QUEEN PELE", THE HAWAIIAN POST OFFICE RECEIVES MANY RETURNED ROCKS FROM THOSE WHO'VE EXPERIENCED MISFORTUNE!

SHIVA

OR SIVA IS ONE OF THREE ASPECTS OF THE HINDU DIVINE ~ THE "TRIMURTI". HE IS **DESTROYER** OR **TRANSFORMER** ALONG WITH CREATOR BRAHMA & PRESERVER VISHNU. HIS NAME MEANS "THE AUSPICIOUS ONE" ~ KIND, FRIENDLY AND GRACIOUS. ~ HE IS HUSBAND TO DIVINE MOTHER **PARVATI**, ALSO KNOWN AS **SHAKTI** - DIVINE ENERGY. (SEE GANESH) HE IS THE SUPREME DEITY IN *SHAIVISM*, A HINDU DENOMINATION.

SHIVA'S DRUM: the SOUND of CEASELESS CREATION

OH THE DIVINE COUPLE SHIVA PARVATI! O! PROTECTORS OF THIS UNIVERSE, WITH LORDS BRAHMA AND VISHNU ~ WE PRAY TO YOU FOR OUR WELL-BEING, PROSPERITY & THE ENLIGHTENMENT OF OUR SOULS.
~ SHIVA PRAYER

MY BODY IS MADE OF **5** MANTRAS ~ FOR **5** ELEMENTS, **5** SENSES, **5** ORGANS OF PERCEPTION, **5** ORGANS OF ACTION.

SACRED **RIVER GANGA** FLOWS FROM MY HAIR TO EARTH, BRINGING PURITY AND FERTILITY!

MY **TRIDENT** WEAPON STANDS FOR **3** POWERS ~ WILL, ACTION, KNOWLEDGE; **3** ASPECTS OF GOD ~ CREATION, DESTRUCTION & PRESERVATION; AND **3** QUALITIES OF NATURE ~ DYNAMIC, STILL & PURE.

ON MY FOREHEAD ARE **3** LINES OF **ASH** ~ WHAT REMAINS WHEN THE PHYSICAL WORLD HAS BEEN BURNT IN THE FIRE OF ENLIGHTENMENT!

MY **SNAKES**, BRINGERS OF DEATH AND REBIRTH, SYMBOLIZE TRANSFORMATION AS THEY SHED THEIR SKINS!

"OM": the SOUND of the UNIVERSE

SHIVA IS "NATARAJA", KING OF **DANCE**, MOVING TO THE RHYTHM OF THE **COSMOS**, DRUMMING CREATION'S SOUND, VICTORIOUSLY STEPPING ON THE DEMON OF IGNORANCE!

WHAT'S THAT **EYE** ON HIS FOREHEAD?

IT'S THE "THIRD EYE"- REPRESENTING SPIRITUAL AND INTUITIVE AWARENESS!

St. Francis of Assisi
1181 to 1226
ITALY
BORN TO A WEALTHY MERCHANT, HE HAD ALL HE COULD DESIRE; UNTIL A VISION OF JESUS LIT HIS SPIRITUAL FIRE...
PAPA... I HAVE NO MORE NEED OF MATERIAL THINGS. I MUST LEAVE HOME TO FOLLOW GOD'S PATH...
FRANCIS! THAT'S RIDICULOUS! DON'T THROW THIS ALL AWAY!
I'M SORRY PAPA...
WELL. DON'T COME BACK THEN. HMPH.
WANDERING HILL AND VALLEY, WITH POVERTY HIS VOW, HELPING POOR AND OUTCAST, BLESSING SHEEP AND COW.
WHAT A KIND HUMAN!
AYE!
SISTER MOON AND BROTHER SUN ~ ALL LIFE HIS DEAR RELATIONS. SINGING PRAISES WITH THE BIRDS FOR ALL OF GOD'S CREATIONS!
ONCE, FRANCIS CAME UPON A WOLF, MENACING A VILLAGE...
MUST FIND LAMB TO EAT! OR SMALL HUMAN!
WAIT! BROTHER WOLF! I KNOW YOU ARE HUNGRY AND THAT IS WHY YOU FRIGHTEN THE VILLAGERS. LET US GO TO THE FOREST AND I WILL FEED YOU. JOIN ME... BE AT PEACE MY BROTHER....
FRANCIS ATTRACTED MANY FOLLOWERS WHO BECAME KNOWN AS THE FRANCISCANS.

Lord, make me an instrument of your **peace**. Where there is hatred, let me sow love; where there is injury, pardon; where there is doubt, faith; where there is despair, hope; where there is darkness, light; & where there is sadness, joy.

Lord, grant that I may not so much seek to be consoled as to console; to be understood as to understand; to be loved as to **love**; for it is in giving that we receive; it is in pardoning that we are pardoned; & it is in dying that we are born to eternal **life**.

~ATTRIBUTED TO ST. FRANCIS

Roman Catholics honor Saint Francis as a blessor of birds and beasts. On October 4th, his feast day (the day of a saint's celebration) ~ children bring their pets to receive his blessing.

Tara

Her name means "Star" in Sanskrit

Buddhism in Tibet ~ ca. 600 CE

Once upon a time in ancient Tibet, a lake was formed from the compassionate tears of a Buddha called Avalokitesvara.* On this lake floated a beautiful golden lotus blossom. Rising from this flower, the *female Buddha* **Tara** first appeared. Because of Tara's *bodhicitta* — awakened and compassionate heart — she had the opportunity to assume human form as a man...

"There are many who wish to achieve enlightenment in a man's form. But few who wish to work for the welfare of all beings in a **female** form. For **all** my lifetimes I vow to be born as a **woman**!"

*The current manifestation of Avalokitesvara is the Dalai Lama, spiritual leader of Tibet

As mother to her children, she smiles with loving face, protects from hurt & danger, folds all in warm embrace.

Tara has twenty-one forms that are aspects of her light — they're virtuous examples for developing insight.

Some of them are...

- *Blue Tara* ~ transmutation of anger
- *Black Tara* ~ power
- *Green Tara* ~ dynamic enlightened activity
- *White Tara* ~ compassion, healing, serenity
- *Yellow Tara* ~ prosperity
- *Red Tara* ~ magnetizing good things

GREEN TARA

...HOMAGE TO YOU, TARA, WHOSE FACE IS LIKE ONE HUNDRED FULL AUTUMN MOONS GATHERED TOGETHER, BLAZING WITH THE EXPANDING LIGHT OF A THOUSAND STARS ASSEMBLED...

...HOMAGE TO YOU, TARA, BORN FROM A GOLDEN BLUE LOTUS, WHOSE HANDS ARE BEAUTIFULLY ADORNED WITH LOTUS FLOWERS, YOU WHO ARE THE EMBODIMENT OF GIVING, JOYOUS EFFORT, ASCETICISM, PEACE, PATIENCE, CONCENTRATION AND PRACTICE...

~ FROM HOMAGE TO THE 21 TARAS

ཨོཾ་མ་ཎི་པདྨེ་ཧཱུྃ

•OM MANI PADME HUM• FAMOUS TIBETAN BUDDHIST MANTRA, INVOKING THE BODHISATTVA OF COMPASSION, AVALOKITESVARA.

ཨོཾ་ཏཱ་རེ་ཏུཏྟཱ་རེ་ཏུ་རེ་སྭཱ་ཧཱ

...AND THAT'S TIBETAN SCRIPT FOR **TARA'S** SPECIAL MANTRA: OM TARE TUTTARE TURE SVAHA.

Virgin of Guadalupe
JUAN DIEGO TWICE VISITS THE BISHOP TO TELL WHAT HE'S SEEN...
IN 1531 MEXICO CITY, AZTEC INDIAN JUAN DIEGO IS HURRYING TO MASS...
JUAN DIEGO!
WHAT?! WHO?..
I AM THE VIRGIN MARY, MOTHER OF GOD. BUILD ME A CHURCH ON THIS SPOT TO REMIND PEOPLE OF MY LOVE WHEN THEY ARE SUFFERING!
AH YES. HMM... WELL... CAN YOU PROVE IT WAS THE HOLY VIRGIN?
BUT... WELL... NO...
NO, NO. WE WILL NOT BUILD A CHURCH.
THE VIRGIN APPEARS TO HIM AGAIN...
PLEASE HEAVENLY LADY, SEND SOMEONE ELSE TO THE BISHOP. HE WON'T LISTEN TO ME!
NO, JUAN DIEGO, YOU ARE THE ONE. TAKE THESE FLOWERS, PUT THEM IN YOUR CLOAK AND GO BACK TO HIM...
MOTHER OF GOD!
HER IMAGE! ON THE CLOAK!
JUAN DIEGO, I'M SORRY I DOUBTED YOU... YES! WE WILL BUILD A CHURCH!

THE VIRGIN OF GUADALUPE HAS COME TO REPRESENT MEXICAN CULTURE, WHICH COMBINES THE WORLD OF THE INDIGENOUS INDIANS OF MEXICO WITH THE WAYS & RELIGION OF THE SPANISH CATHOLICS. SOME SAY THE SPOT WHERE THE VIRGIN APPEARED WAS THE SITE OF A SHRINE TO THE LOCAL EARTH GODDESS, TONANTZIN.

"LA VIRGINCITA" ~ THE LITTLE VIRGIN ~ AS HER PEOPLE AFFECTIONATELY CALL HER, IS MEXICO CITY'S PATRON SAINT. JUAN DIEGO'S CLOAK, STILL MARKED WITH HER IMAGE, RESTS IN THE BASILICA OF GUADALUPE BEHIND BULLETPROOF GLASS.

"CUIDA MI CAMINO"
"CARE FOR MY PATH"
~ WORDS UNDER HER IMAGE, PAINTED ON THE SIDE OF A CAR IN CALIFORNIA

YAHWEH

ORIGINALLY A GOD OF *POLYTHEISTIC* SUMERIA, THE NAME *YAHWEH* WAS CLAIMED BY THE HEBREWS FOR THEIR ONE & ONLY DEITY. GOD OF THE HEBREW SCRIPTURES, THE NAMES "ELOHIM", "ADONAI" & "SHADDAI" ALSO REFER TO HIM. WRITTEN HEBREW HAS NO VOWELS; THE FOUR HEBREW LETTERS OF HIS NAME CORRESPOND TO **YHWH**. ADDING VOWELS MAKES IT EASIER TO SAY. "JEHOVAH" IS ANOTHER VERSION MADE BY ADDING DIFFERENT VOWELS: **YAHOWAH**. RELIGIOUS JEWS CONSIDER THE NAME OF GOD SO **HOLY** IT SHOULD NOT BE PRONOUNCED AT ALL!

LIKE MUSLIMS, JEWS BELIEVE IT'S NOT RIGHT TO DEPICT GOD'S FACE. THE *TORAH*'S GOD REVEALS HIMSELF THROUGH SIGNS...

WHO ARE YOU?!

I AM THAT I AM!

WHOA!

THE PROPHET MOSES WAS TENDING SHEEP WHEN HE SAW A BUSH AFIRE. BUT THE BUSH WAS NOT CONSUMED BY FLAMES — FOR IT WAS **GOD** IN THAT MIRACLE PYRE!

YAHWEH IS THE SAME GOD WORSHIPPED BY CHRISTIANS AND MUSLIMS (SEE ALLAH) — WHOSE RELIGIONS ALSO DESCEND FROM THE HEBREW PROPHET ABRAHAM. CHRISTIANS CALL YAHWEH "GOD THE FATHER" OR JEHOVAH — ONE OF THE HOLY TRINITY. BUT A THREE-PART GOD GOES AGAINST JEWISH AND MUSLIM *MONOTHEISM*.

EUROPEAN CHRISTIAN ARTISTS HAVE OFTEN DEPICTED GOD THE FATHER AS AN OLD WHITE MAN WITH LONG BEARD...

MAMA, WHAT COLOR IS GOD?

THE SAME COLOR AS **WATER**!

CREATION!

EVOLUTION!

BOTH!

WHATEVER!

SOME KNOW GOD MADE THE WORLD IN SEVEN DAYS, SOME KNOW EVOLUTION IS TRUE. SOME INSIST WE SHOULD ALL AGREE: ON ITS AWESOMENESS — WE DO!

BLESSED ARE YOU, LORD, OUR GOD, KING OF THE UNIVERSE, WHO BRINGS FORTH BREAD FROM THE EARTH.
~JEWISH BLESSING BEFORE EATING BREAD

WHAT IS YAHWEH LIKE?

REKNOWNED 12TH CENTURY JEWISH PHILOSOPHER MAIMONIDES BELIEVED THAT TO DESCRIBE GOD IN HUMAN TERMS BELITTLES HIM!

SPEAKING OF JUDAISM, WHAT *IS* HANUKKAH?

IT'S THE 8 DAY "FESTIVAL OF LIGHTS", CELEBRATING THE REDEDICATION OF JERUSALEM'S SACRED TEMPLE IN 2ND CENTURY BCE.

BOTH HANUKKAH & CHRISTMAS COINCIDED WITH MORE ANCIENT WINTER **SOLSTICE** CELEBRATIONS!

WHY AREN'T THERE **SAINTS** IN JUDAISM?

BECAUSE THE FOCUS IS ON THE JEWISH PEOPLE AS A **WHOLE** RATHER THAN INDIVIDUALS~ THOUGH THERE ARE HISTORICAL MODELS OF INSPIRATION, INCLUDING ABRAHAM, ELIJAH, ESTHER & RUTH. (SEE MOSES)

Yemaya

Great Mother Ocean, Goddess of African Yoruba tradition, she did not desert her people when they were enslaved in the Americas. Today she's particularly popular in Brazil, where she's called **IEMANJA**. She is one of the 7 Orishas and is honored in Cuba, parts of Latin America, the Caribbean & the U.S.A. — wherever Santería is practiced. (See Chango)

Like water, Yemaya is both constant & changing. Originally a Nigerian river deity, she became goddess of the seas when her people were aboard the slave ships.

She's the womb of all creation, mother of secrets & dreams!

Hold a seashell to your ear & you can hear her voice!

Watermelon is her fruit, bubbles & foam her lace, dolphins & fish her children, moon her changeable face!

She carves a mighty canyon with waterfalls and tide, she washes away each heartache with embrace that's deep & wide!

> O MOTHER OF WATERS!
> GREAT IS YOUR POWER, YOUR STRENGTH & YOUR LIGHT...
> LET YOUR GREATNESS BE THE
> GREATEST WEALTH YOU DISPENSE TO ME...
> SURROUNDED BY SWEET MELODIES
> SPRINGING FROM YOUR OWN SELF...
> ~ PRAYER TO YEMAYA

YEMAYA IS ESPECIALLY RESPONSIVE TO WOMEN & GIRLS. THE BEACH IS A POWERFUL PLACE TO ENLIST HER ASSISTANCE. DIG A SPOT IN THE SAND FOR BLUE OR WHITE CANDLES, LIGHT THEM & MAKE YOUR REQUEST. ENTER THE WATER, GREET YEMAYA & PLACE 7 WHITE ROSES IN THE SEA. IMMERSE YOURSELF 7 TIMES!

"ZOROASTER" IS GREEK FOR: # ZARATHUSTRA

I AM THE *FARAVAHAR*, ICON OF ZOROASTRIANISM. I SYMBOLIZE THE IMMORTAL **SOUL**.

BORN IN PERSIA (NOW IRAN) INTO THE *POLYTHEISTIC* RELIGION OF MITHRA, HE WAS A COURT PROPHET & POET. HE MAY HAVE LIVED AS EARLY AS 1500 BCE, BUT THE ZOROASTRIAN CALENDAR DATES FROM 630 BCE, TRADITIONALLY THE YEAR OF HIS **VISION**...

ONE EVENING, ZARATHUSTRA WATCHED A BRILLIANT SUN SET BEYOND THE MOUNTAINS...

BEHOLD! NOW! BATTLE OF LIGHT & DARK! GOOD & EVIL! ANGELS & DEVILS!

WHA?... WHO? ARE YOU?!

I AM *AHURA MAZDA*, THE **ONE** WISE LORD!

HOW CAN I BE SPEAKING **DIRECTLY** WITH **GOD**?!

I NEED NO SPOKESPERSON! MY TEMPLE IS NOT MADE OF BRICK OR STONE ~ IT IS IN THE HEARTS & SOULS OF PEOPLE! YOU ARE MY **COWORKERS**! CHOOSE WISELY IN THIS LIFE: **GOOD THOUGHTS, WORDS AND DEEDS**.

ZARATHUSTRA SHARED HIS INSIGHTS THROUGH TEACHING AND WRITING. HIS FOLLOWING GREW AND THE RELIGION OF **ZOROASTRIANISM** WAS BORN. AN EARLY FORM OF MONOTHEISM, ITS IDEAS — A FUTURE SAVIOR, LAST JUDGMENT AND RESURRECTION OF THE BODY — APPEARED AGAIN LATER IN CHRISTIANITY. ~ BECAUSE ZOROASTRIANS WERE PERSECUTED IN 9TH CENTURY PERSIA, MANY MOVED TO INDIA, WHERE THEY ARE KNOWN AS "PARSEES" ("PERSIANS"). ~ THEIR SCRIPTURE IS THE "AVESTA" WHICH CONTAINS THE "GATHARS" — HYMNS BY ZARATHUSTRA.

WHAT IS "THUS SPAKE ZARATHUSTRA"?

A WORK BY 19TH CENTURY PHILOSOPHER NIETZSCHE — HE USED THE PROPHET'S MOUTH TO EXPOUND HIS OWN BELIEF: THAT GOD IS DEAD.

A FLAME BURNS CONTINUOUSLY IN ZOROASTRIAN TEMPLES. "THE **SACRED FIRE** IS A SYMBOL OF THE WISE LORD'S PRESENCE AS WE GATHER TO WORSHIP. HE IS WARMTH, PEACE & ENLIGHTENMENT."
~WORSHIPPER IN IRAN

Glossary

amulet an object used as a charm against evil or injury
angel a being that is an intermediary between heaven and earth
asceticism the practice of leading a life of extreme simplicity
atheist one who denies the existence of God
avatar an incarnation
BCE Before the Common Era
bhakti devotion
bodhisattva an enlightened being who, out of compassion, forgoes nirvana in order to save others
ca. circa; about
caste hereditary social classes of traditional Hindu society
CE the Common Era; begins with year 0 (birth of Christ)
chakra one of seven centers of spiritual energy in the body, according to Indian yoga philosophy
crucify put to death by being nailed to a cross
deity a god or goddess
demon an evil supernatural being; for Hindus, it is also a shape-changer and illusionist
devil an evil spirit; enemy of God
disciple one who embraces and assists in spreading the teachings of another
enlightenment spiritual insight
evangelical Protestant churches that stress personal spiritual transformation and the absolute truth of the Bible
fundamentalism a movement marked by rigid adherence to basic principles
god a being of supernatural powers, believed in or worshiped by people; monotheists spell with a capital G
goddess female god
guru a revered teacher or mentor
heaven the home of God, angels, and the souls of the dead
hell the home of devils and condemned souls
hypothesis a tentative explanation that accounts for a set of facts
iconography the use of symbols or images that are recognized to have particular meaning
idol an image used as an object of worship
immortal not subject to death
incarnation the condition of having bodily form
indigenous originating in an area; native
karma the effect of one's actions and conduct during successive phases of existence
Mahabharata a sacred epic poem of the Hindus, originally written in Sanskrit
mantra sacred words repeated in prayer or meditation
Mass the celebration of the Eucharist, in which bread and wine, symbolizing the body and blood of Jesus, are consecrated and consumed in remembrance of Jesus's death
matter that which occupies space and can be perceived by the senses; the physical universe
meditate in Buddhism or Hinduism, to train or empty the mind, as by focusing on the breath, a single object, or a mantra
messiah an expected savior or liberator
monotheism the belief that there is only one God
monotheist one who believes in only one God
mosque a Muslim house of worship
nirvana the ultimate state of being in which one has attained detached wisdom and compassion
original sin in Christian theology, the belief that everyone is born sinful because of Adam's (the first man, according to the Bible) original disobedience to God
orthodox relating to the most traditional or conservative form of a religion or ideology
pagan one who practices nature-based spirituality; a person of non Judeo-Christian monotheistic orientation
pantheism identifying the deity with the universe
pantheon all the gods of a people
piety devotion and reverence, especially to God
polytheism worship of or belief in more than one god
prophet a person who speaks by, or as if by, divine inspiration
Ramayana a classical Hindu epic, originally written in Sanskrit
reincarnation rebirth of the soul in another body
ritual a ceremonial act or a series of such acts
rosary a series of prayers dedicated to Mary; string of beads on which the prayers are counted
sacred worthy of religious veneration; made or declared holy

sage a greatly respected wise person
saint a person considered holy and worthy of great public respect or reverence
Sanskrit an ancient Indic language that is the classical language of India
shrine a container for sacred objects or a site revered for its associations
sin a breaking of a religious or moral law
soul the animating force within living beings
spirit a supernatural being; soul
St. abbreviation for "Saint"
temple a building dedicated to religious ceremonies or worship
transcendent in spiritual context, rising above common thought or ideas; exalted, mystical

Resources

Beer, Robert. *Handbook of Tibetan Buddhist Symbols*. Boston; Shambhala 2003
Chodron, Pema. *Comfortable With Uncertainty*. Boston: Shambhala 2008
Dunn-Mascetti, Manuela. *Saints—the Chosen Few*. New York: Ballantine 1994
Dunnington, Jacqueline Orsini. *Celebrating Guadalupe*. Tucson, Arizona: Rio Nuevo Pub. 2004
Edwards, Carolyn McVickar. *Return of the Light*. New York: Marlowe & Co. 2000
_____. *Storyteller's Goddess*. New York; Marlowe & Co. 2000
Griffith, Jim. *Saints of the Southwest*. Tucson, Arizona Rio Nuevo Publishers 2000
Illes, Judika. *The Element Encyclopedia of 5000 Spells*. London: HarperCollins 2004
_____. *The Element Encyclopedia of Witchcraft*. London: HarperCollins 2005
Jackson, David & Janice. *Tibetan Thangka Painting*. Ithaca, NY: Snow Lion Publications 1984
Lundy, Miranda. *Sacred Geometry*. New York: Walker & Company 1998
Majupuria, T.C. & Kumar, Rojit. *Gods and Goddesses*. India: Smt. M. D. Gupta 1998
O'Donnell, Kevin. *Inside World Religions*. Minneapolis: Fortress Press 2007
Roberts, Elizabeth & Amidon, Elias. *Earth Prayers*. New York: Harper Collins 1991
Ryan, M. J. *A Grateful Heart*. Berkeley: Conari Press 2002
Seiden, Allan. *The Art of the Hula*. Hawaii: Island Heritage Publishing 1999
Smith, Huston. *The Illustrated World's Religions*. New York: Harper Collins 1991
Teish, Luisah. *Jambalaya*. San Francisco: Harper & Row 1985

There are countless web sites with information about religions; here are a few:

about.com
acdagy.com *African Cultural and Development Association*
afrikaworld.net
answers.com
bahai.com
bahai.us
bahaiprayers.org
beliefnet.com *spiritual exploration*
bibleorigins.net
goddess.ws
himalayanacademy.com
historywiz.com
hulapreservation.org
islamfortoday.com
mahashivratri.org *Society for Confluence of Festivals in India*
purifymind.com *Buddhism*
religionfacts.com
religioustolerance.org
religiousworlds.com
sacred-texts.com
sikh-history.com
sikh.org
sikhcoalition.org
spaceandmotion.com *philosophy*
understanding-islam.com
zoroaster.net

About the Author

Kathleen Edwards has a long history of combining writing with visual art, and she often incorporates writing and poetry into custom made works. Her drawings and paintings have graced book covers and interiors, calendars, and greeting cards. Her clients include HarperCollins, Chronicle Books, Conari Press, and Tarcher Putnam.

Her fine art paintings and sculptures have been widely exhibited at many venues including the San Francisco Museum of Modern Art Artists Gallery, the Oakland Museum, the Vancouver Museum, and the San Francisco Craft and Folk Art Museum.

Edwards studied at the Pratt Institute in New York City and later completed her Master's degree in Interdisciplinary Arts at San Francisco State University. She has won awards from Bookbuilder's West and the San Francisco Society of Illustrators.

Edwards lives with her husband in San Anselmo, California.